MY MUNCH BOOK

by
Gretchen Bartlett

and
Luann Williams

artist
Ray Packard

MY MUNCH BOOK
Copyright © 1981
Gretchen Bartlett
Luann Williams
Artist - Ray Packard

Copyright Registration number TX783878

Published by:
Nourishing Thoughts
Enterprises
P.O. Box 1402
Hudson, Ohio 44236

First Edition - 1981 Second Edition - 1982

Printed in the United States of America
Printed by Hudson Printing, Hudson, Ohio
ISBN 0-9601198-2-5 795

DEDICATED TO...

CARL AND LUCILE HORST
whose creative fruit and
vegetable gardens are
an inspiration from an
educational and
healthful view.

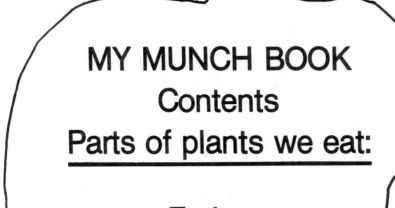

MY MUNCH BOOK

Contents

Parts of plants we eat:

Fruits
Leaves
Stems
Flowers
Roots
Seeds

We eat many parts of plants: fruits, leaves, stems, roots, flowers, and seeds.

Some munch foods to eat -

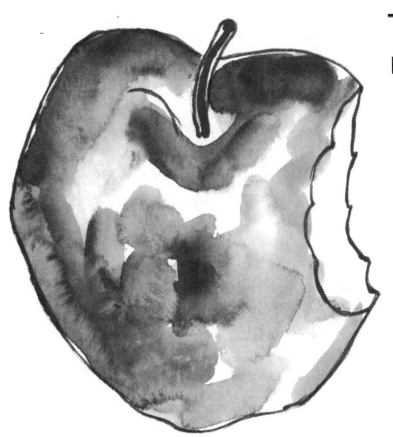

Apples grow on trees.

They crunch when we munch them.

Apples are yellow, red, or green.

Peaches feel fuzzy. They are juicy inside.
Peaches have very hard seeds.

Nectarines are like
peaches without
the fuzz.

Grapefruits are yellow or pink.
Oranges are orange in color.

Tangerines are like oranges with loose skins and sections that peel.

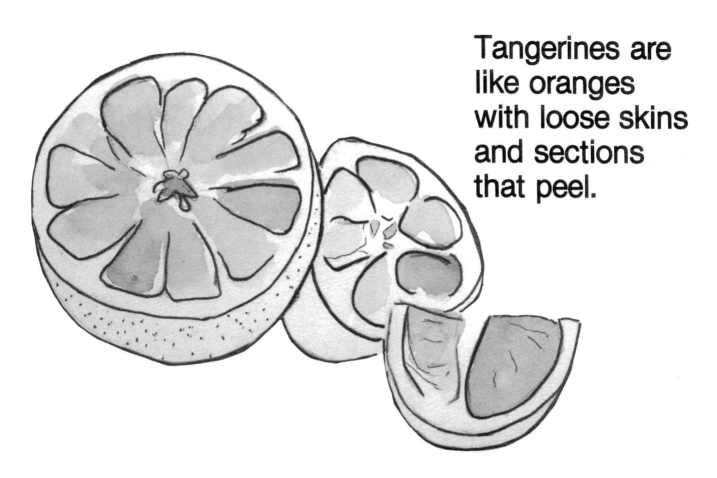

Lemons and limes taste sour.

Limes are green.   Lemons are yellow.

Pears can have yellow, red, or green skins. They are white inside.

Cherries are red, yellow, or black.
They have very hard, round, smooth seeds.

Avocados have thick, dark skins and soft, light green insides. They have a big, hard, brown seed.

Plums are purple, red, or green.
They are juicy inside and have
a hard seed.

Prunes are dried plums.

A mango has a skin that can be orange, pink, or green.

Mangos are orange inside with a large, flat seed.

A papaya is orange inside and outside.
It has small, black seeds.

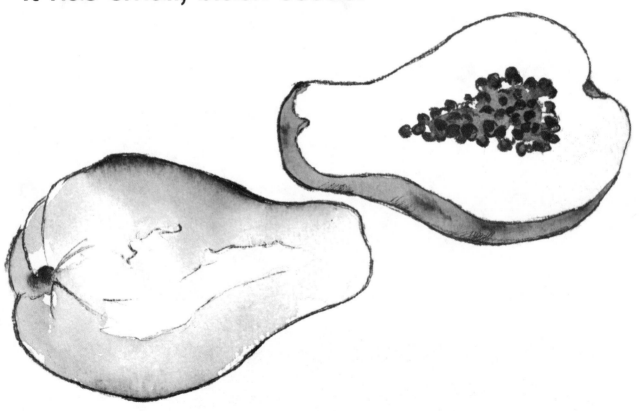

Bananas grow in bunches. They are yellow or red. Bananas have thick skins and are soft inside.

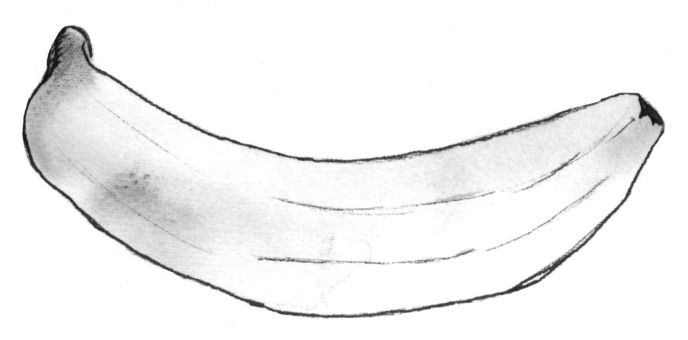

Pineapples are juicy,
yellow, and sweet.
The juice is good
to drink.

Berries grow on vines and bushes.
Strawberries are red and have tiny seeds
on the outside.

Most berries have bumpy lumps, but blueberries are smooth.

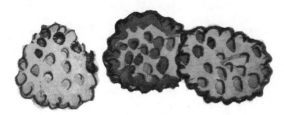

red or yellow raspberries

black raspberries

blueberries

Kiwi fruits are berries. They are fuzzy and brown outside. Inside they are green with very tiny, black seeds.

Melons grow on vines. Some watermelons are large and green. They are red and juicy inside.

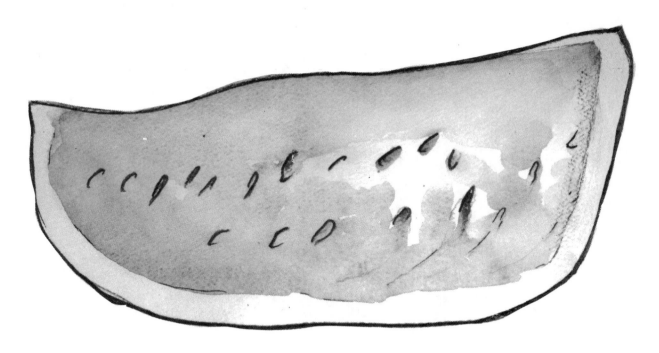

Cantaloupe and honeydew are both melons.

They have many seeds. Cantaloupe is orange inside; honeydew is light green.

Grapes are green, red, or purple.

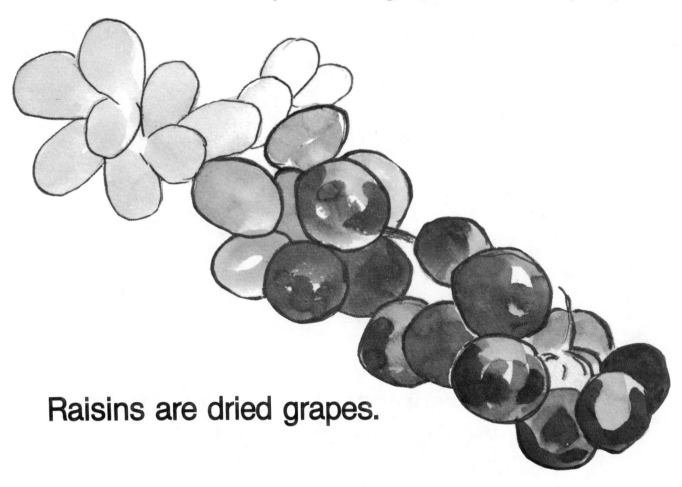

Raisins are dried grapes.

Tomatoes are shiny and smooth on the outside.
Ripe tomatoes are usually red, yellow, or orange.

There are many kinds of squash with different shapes, sizes, and colors.

They may be: short, fat, long, skinny, round, scalloped, crooknecked, or pear shaped.

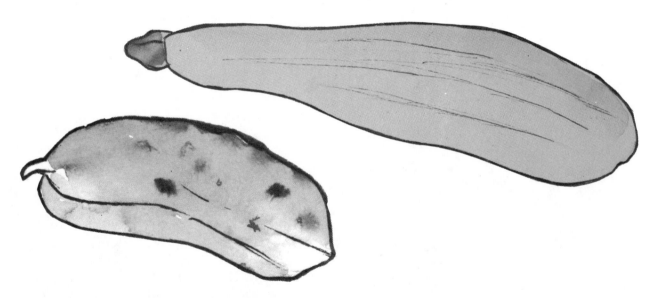

Squash may be green, yellow, white, or orange.

There are many leafy vegetables. We eat the leaves of the spinach and parsley plants.

Both of these leaves are green.

Spearmint and peppermint leaves are green.

They can be used to add flavor to foods.

They smell like mint.

Leaf lettuce is usually green.
Some lettuce leaves are dark
red in color.

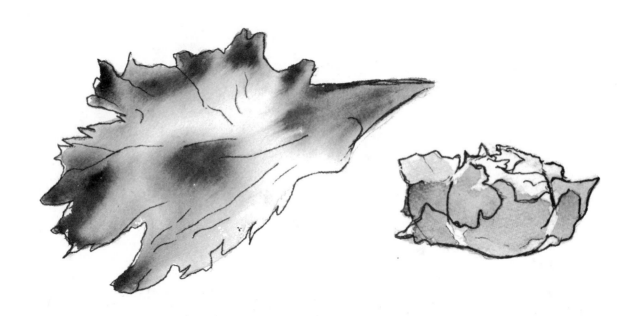

Head lettuce leaves fold into round shapes.

A cabbage has many leaves that fold to make a hard head. Cabbage can be green, purple, or white. It tastes good raw or cooked.

Brussels sprouts are leaves. They look and taste like tiny cabbages.

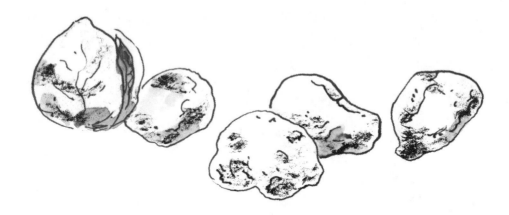

We eat the stems of some plants.

The young tips of the asparagus stem are tender to eat. They are green or white.

Rhubarb has a red stem.

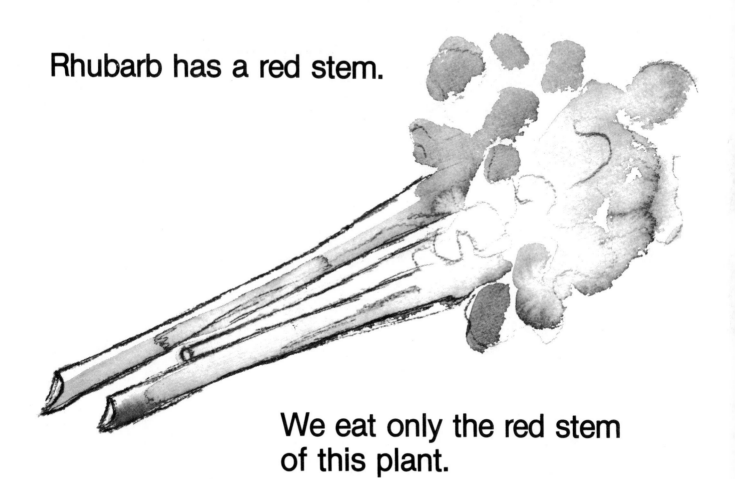

We eat only the red stem
of this plant.

We eat the stems and leaves of the celery plant. The crunchy stem is white or green.

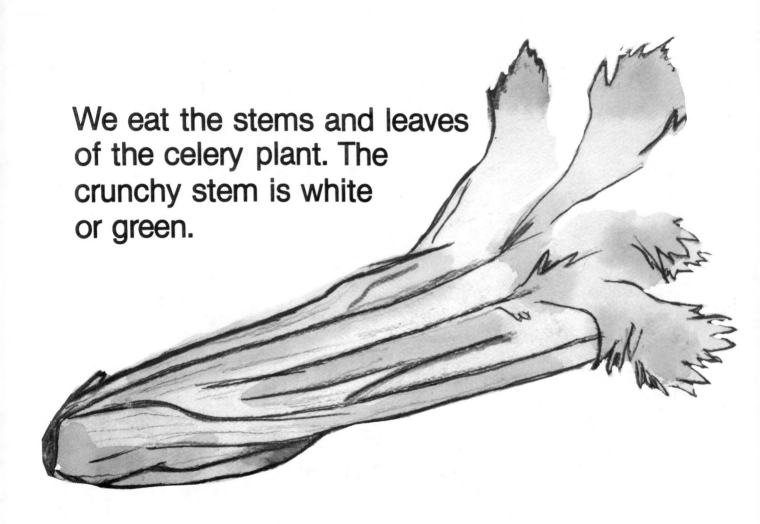

We eat the flowers of some plants.

The cauliflower has a white flower.
It is good to eat raw or cooked.

Broccoli plants have green flowers. We eat the leaves, stems, and buds of the plant.

Broccoli buds look like tiny green trees. They are good raw or cooked.

Artichokes are plants with very large flower buds. We eat the inner parts of the bud.

We eat the roots of
some plants. They
grow underground.

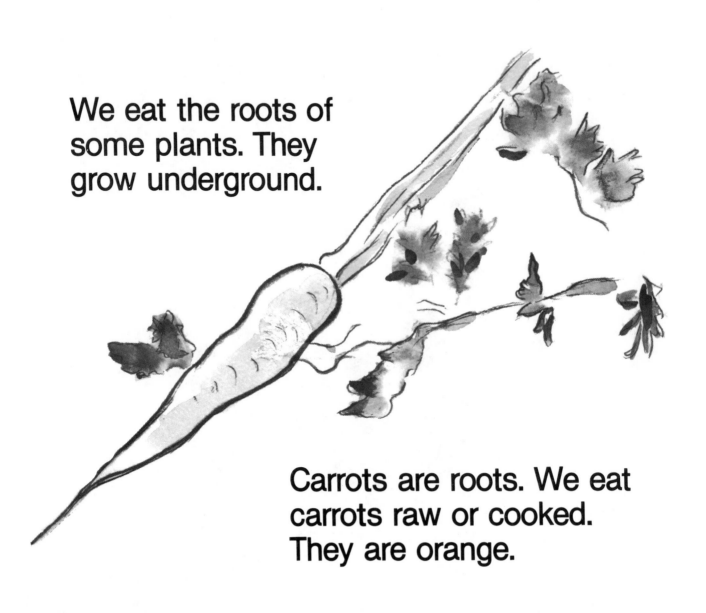

Carrots are roots. We eat
carrots raw or cooked.
They are orange.

Radishes are roots. They make
a loud crunch when they are munched.
Most radishes are red or white roots.

We eat the leaves and roots of beets.

They taste good raw or cooked. Beets are red.

Turnips are white and purple.
The roots and leaves are good
cooked.

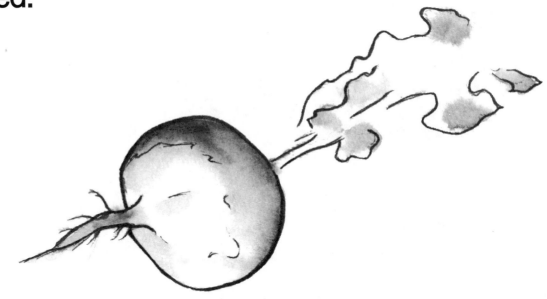

Potatoes are swollen roots.
Regular potatoes are white inside.

Sweet potatoes and yams
are orange inside.

We eat pumpkin seeds
and sunflower seeds.

They are good
raw or roasted.
Chew them well.

Sprouts are seeds that start to grow.

Alfalfa and mung bean sprouts are good to eat.
There are many other sprouts that are good, too.

There are many kinds of peas.
Peas are seeds.

Peas taste good cooked or raw. They grow
in a pod on a vine. Sometimes we eat
the pod.

There are many kinds of beans. They are seeds. We eat the pods of some beans.

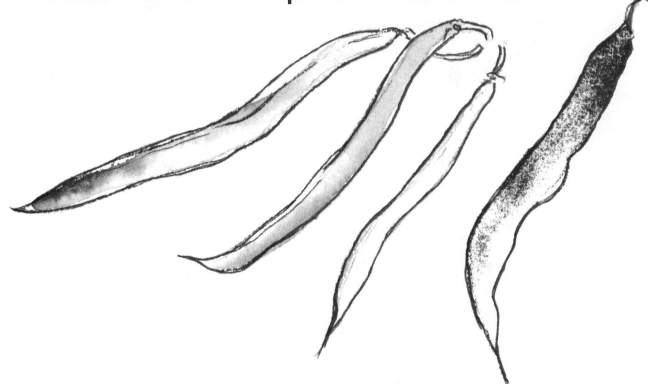

Beans have many shapes, colors, and names. Green beans, lima beans, navy beans, and kidney beans are some common beans.

Grains are seeds.
They can be: rice, barley,
wheat, oats, rye, buckwheat,
corn, and millet.
We eat grains in cereals
and breads.

We eat the seeds of corn.

Some special corn kernels
pop when heated.
They turn into popcorn.

Corn can be munched on or off the cob.

Nuts have hard shells. Nuts are seeds.
Chew the inside of nuts carefully.

Walnuts, almonds, pecans, Brazil nuts,
filberts, pistachios, hickory, and
chestnuts are nuts we eat.

A coconut has a very hard shell.
We drink the liquid and eat the white
inner part.

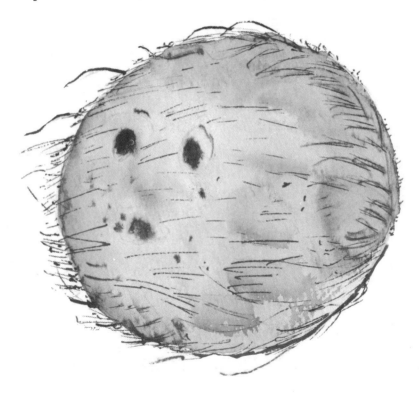

Plan a munch party with a friend or by yourself.

My MUNCH Party

Creative Recipes
and Activities.

MY MUNCH PARTY
Contents

Plan a munch party with friends.

Plan foods to eat:

1.
2.
3.
4.
5.
6.
7.
8.
9.
10.

Plan things to do:

1.
2.
3.
4.
5.
6.
7.
8.
9.
10.

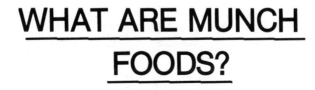

WHAT ARE MUNCH FOODS?

Munch foods are snack foods.

Munch foods are good for us to eat.

Munch foods are tasty.

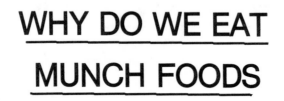

WHY DO WE EAT

MUNCH FOODS

They are good.
They give us energy.
They make us strong.
They help us think.
They keep us healthy.

WHERE DO WE FIND
MUNCH FOODS?

Trees
Bushes
Vines
Gardens
A food market
In the refrigerator

We find munch foods on trees.

We find munch foods
on bushes and vines.

Most munch foods are found in gardens.

We can buy munch foods at a food market.

Most munch foods are kept
in the refrigerator.

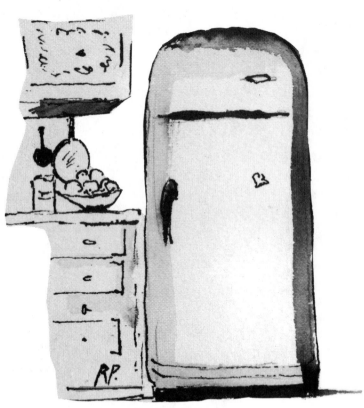

FOODS AND RECIPES

Fresh fruits
 and juices
Dried fruits
Ice fruit pops
Raw vegetables
Sprouts
Party snacks
Peanut butter pieces
Mint tea

Wash and rinse fruits
and vegetables very
carefully.
Wash and rinse the soil
and sprays away.

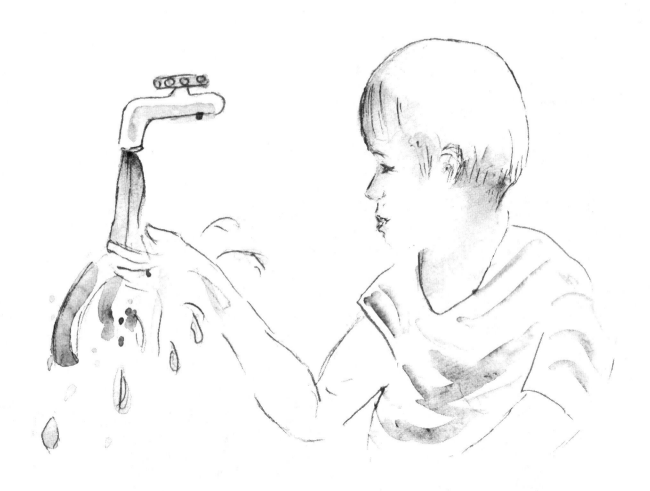

Prepare foods with clean hands.

FRUIT BASKET

- Wash fruits carefully.
- Put fruits in a basket or bowl.

* Fruits make good juices to drink.

FRUIT BALLS

- Cut dried fruit (raisins, prunes, bananas, apricots, pineapples, dates) into small pieces.

- Form them into small balls of fruit.

- To keep fruit balls from being sticky, roll them in oats, sesame seeds, or coconut flakes.

ICE FRUIT POPS

- Pour fruit juice into paper cups or an ice cube tray.
- Set sticks into each cup or cube.
- Freeze.
- Mint leaves may be added.

VEGETABLE BOUQUET

- Wash vegetables carefully.
- Put vegetables in a basket or on a plate.

* Vegetables make good juices to drink.

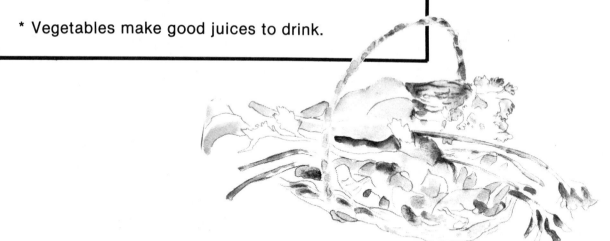

SPROUTS

- Put 2 spoonfuls of seeds in a jar, such as alfalfa or mung beans.
- Fill the jar with water and let them soak overnight.
- In the morning pour off the water.
- Rinse the seeds 3 times everyday.
- Set the jar on its side, so the seeds are not crowded.
- Sprouts will be two inches long and ready to eat in 5 days.
- Keep sprouted seeds in the refrigerator.

PARTY SNACKS

Fill a bowl or basket with
seeds, nuts, and dried fruits,
such as: sunflower and pumpkin seeds,
almonds, walnuts, raisins, dates, prunes,
or figs.

PEANUT BUTTER PIECES

- Form peanut butter with your hands to make different shapes.

- Cover all sides with oats, sesame seeds, or shredded coconut.

- Store in the refrigerator.

* Seeds and nuts may be blended with the peanuts.
If the mixture is too stiff, add vegetable oil.

* Ask a grown person to help blend seeds and nuts or to add oil

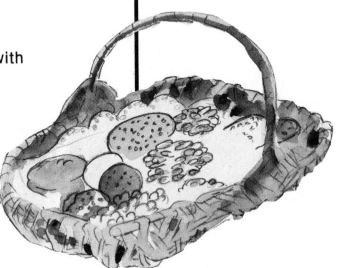

MINT TEA

- Pick fresh mint leaves. (3 - 4 inch sprigs)
- Place leaves and water in a quart bottle.
- Let the bottle with the leaves
    sit in the sun for two hours.
- Serve hot or pour over ice.
- Add a slice of orange, lime, or
    lemon.

Plan to be all ready for the munch party.

OUR SENSES ENJOY A

MUNCH PARTY.

Look at foods.
Touch the foods.
Smell the foods.
Taste the foods.
Hear the foods.

LOOK AT THE FOODS

Look at the munch foods.
Find all the big foods. Find all the
small foods.
They can be put in order from small
to large.
What shapes and colors are the foods?
They can be placed in groups of
red, yellow, or green.

The colors, sizes, and shapes of foods
can remind us of many things.

TOUCH THE FOODS

Touch the munch foods. How do they feel?
What foods feel smooth?
What foods feel bumpy?
What foods feel fuzzy?

Feel the different shapes of foods.
Feel the inside and outside of different foods.

SMELL THE FOODS

Smell the munch foods. Pick them up.
Bite them open. Notice how they smell.
Which smells the strongest?
What smells the best?
What food has very little smell?

Smells can help us remember things. .

HEAR THE FOODS

Bite into the munch foods.
Listen to the foods as you munch them.
Are they loud?
Are they soft?
Does the food crunch or
crackle?
Is it quiet to chew?

Crunch, crunch, crunch until the sounds
are soft or not at all.

TASTE THE FOODS

Each food has its own taste.
What foods taste sweet?
What foods taste sour?
Does the taste change as
the foods are munched?

Munch a crunchy apple.

Alfalfa sprouts
have a quiet crunch.

Eat many different munch foods to have a healthy body.

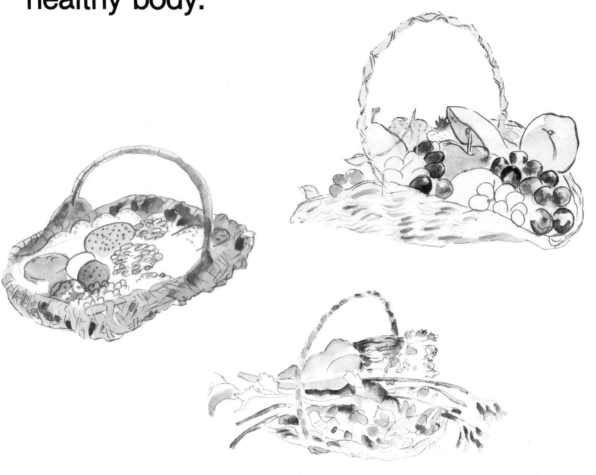

fruits - leaves - stems - roots - flowers - seeds

Draw munch foods for each word:
soft, hard, rough, juicy, crispy, and bumpy.

trees - bushes - vines

trees - bushes - vines

fruits - leaves - stems - roots - flowers - seeds

apples - peaches - grapefruits - oranges - lemons - grapes

Draw some munch fruits:

kiwis - melons - grapes - tomatoes - squash

limes - pears - cherries -avocados - peaches

plums- mangos - papayas - bananas - papayas - pineapples - berries beets - carrots - radishes - turnips - potatoes - lettuce - mint

Draw some munch vegetables:

asparagus - rhubarb - celery - carrots - turnips

cauliflower - broccoli - artichoke - potatoes

spinach - parsley - lettuce - mint - cabbage - brussels sprouts

SEEDS: pumpkin - sunflower -alfalfa - peas - bean sprouts

Draw some seeds and nuts:

NUTS: Brazil - pistachios - hickory - chestnut

NUTS: walnut - almond - pecan - filbert - coconut

GRAINS: corn - rice - barley - oats - rye - wheat - rye - millet - rye

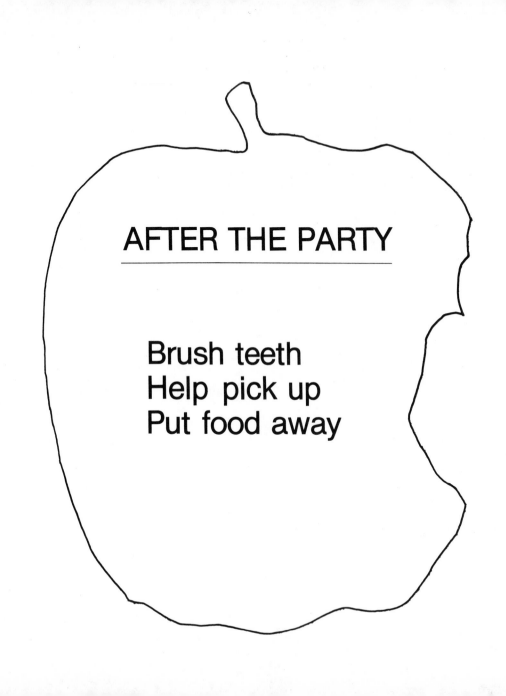

AFTER THE PARTY

Brush teeth
Help pick up
Put food away

Fruit balls and peanut butter
pieces stick to the teeth.

Drink water after
eating to help
clean the mouth.

Brush your teeth
as soon as possible
after eating.

Everything needs to be picked up
after a munch party, so...

...clean up after the munch party.

Be sure all foods are put away
in the kitchen or...

...put leftover food scraps
in the compost, then...

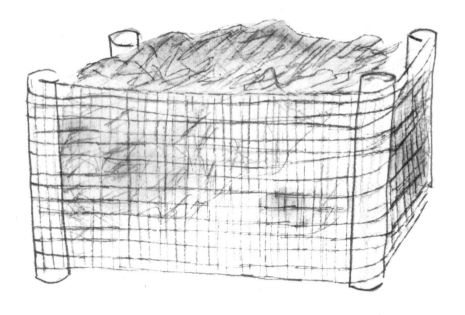

Plan another munch party.

Many thanks to the models who posed for the paintings in MY MUNCH BOOK.

Jennifer Houston

Andrew McCLAIN

Sylvia R. Harris

Christopher Houston

THANK YOU:

Photography	- John H. Ashley
Art & Script	- Sara Criss, Pamela Foti, Dorothy Lerner, Ann Manning, Evelyn Paratore, Katherine Oana
Teachers	Carol Barker, Beatrice Connelly, Vicki Davis
Parents	Harold & Elinor Houston
	Rick & Peggy Law
	James & Debra Marky
	Bradley & Patricia McClain

Consultants:

Dentist	- F.R. Freshley
Creative Ed.	- Alexandria Gombar
Psychologist	- Robert O. Kirkhart
Horticulture	- William L. Snyder
Pediatrician	- F.J. Waickman
Agriculture	- Peter J. Wotowiec

To order MY MUNCH BOOK:

Please return this order form and your
check for $7.95 per book including
shipping and handling to:

MY MUNCH BOOK
P.O. Box 1402
Hudson, Ohio 44236
(216) 686-2662

NAME _____   PHONE _____

ADDRESS_____

CITY _____ STATE _____ ZIP _____

Regular trade discount applies on 3 or more copies.

To order MY MUNCH BOOK:

Please return this order form and your
check for $7.95 per book including
shipping and handling to:

MY MUNCH BOOK
P.O. Box 1402
Hudson, Ohio 44236
(216) 686-2662

NAME _____   PHONE _____

ADDRESS_____

CITY _____ STATE _____ ZIP _____

Regular trade discount applies on 3 or more copies.